Piano Solo

RAGTIME GOSPEL HYMNS

ARRANGED BY STEVEN K. TEDESCO

T0066051

ISBN 978-1-4234-5643-8

HAL•LEONARD®
CORPORATION

7777 W. BLUEMOUND RD. P.O. BOX 13819 MILWAUKEE, WI 53213

In Australia Contact:
Hal Leonard Australia Pty. Ltd.
4 Lentara Court
Cheltenham, Victoria, 3192 Australia

ARE YOU WASHED IN THE BLOOD?

Words and Music by
ELISHA A. HOFFMAN
Arranged by Steven K. Tedesco

AT CALVARY

Words by WILLIAM R. NEWELL
Music by DANIEL B. TOWNER
Arranged by Steven K. Tedesco

Moderately fast

Both hands 8va

DOWN AT THE CROSS
(Glory to His Name)

Words by ELISHA A. HOFFMAN
Music by JOHN H. STOCKTON
Arranged by Steven K. Tedesco

FOOTSTEPS OF JESUS

Words by MARY B.C. SLADE
Music by ASA B. EVERETT
Arranged by Steven K. Tedesco

HE KEEPS ME SINGING

Words and Music by
LUTHER B. BRIDGERS
Arranged by Steven K. Tedesco

JUST A CLOSER WALK WITH THEE

Traditional
Arranged by Steven K. Tedesco

Moderately slow

LEANING ON THE EVERLASTING ARMS

Words by ELISHA A. HOFFMAN
Music by ANTHONY J. SHOWALTER
Arranged by Steven K. Tedesco

With energy

PRECIOUS MEMORIES

Words and Music by
J.B.F. WRIGHT
Arranged by Steven K. Tedesco

SINCE JESUS CAME INTO MY HEART

Words by RUFUS H. McDANIEL
Music by CHARLES H. GABRIEL
Arranged by Steven K. Tedesco

Dedicated with love to my supportive wife, Kristina

STANDING ON THE PROMISES

Words and Music by R. KELSO CARTER
Arranged by Steven K. Tedesco

SWEET BY AND BY

Words by SANFORD FILLMORE BENNETT
Music by JOSEPH P. WEBSTER
Arranged by Steven K. Tedesco

Dedicated to my mother, Jeannette Tedesco

WHAT A FRIEND WE HAVE IN JESUS

Words by JOSEPH M. SCRIVEN
Music by CHARLES C. CONVERSE
Arranged by Steven K. Tedesco

WHEN THE ROLL IS CALLED UP YONDER

Words and Music by
JAMES M. BLACK
Arranged by Steven K. Tedesco

WHEN WE ALL GET TO HEAVEN

Words by ELIZA E. HEWITT
Music by EMILY D. WILSON
Arranged by Steven K. Tedesco

A NEW NAME IN GLORY

Words and Music by
C. AUSTIN MILES
Arranged by Steven K. Tedesco